This book belongs to

Freya Lucy King

The Usborne
Horse and Pony Treasury

Rosie Dickins and Leonie Pratt

Illustrated by Norman Young
and Barry Ablett

Designed by Doriana Berkovic
Edited by Lesley Sims

With thanks to Juliet Penwarden, BHS II,
for her expert advice

Contents

Famous horses in life and art

Myths and stories

All about horses

All kinds of horses

People have been falling in love with horses and ponies for centuries. These animals have something for everyone – whether it's the natural grace of a horse or the mischievous character of a riding school pony.

Horses and ponies are slightly different kinds of the same animal. Ponies are stockier and more bouncy to ride. Horses are taller and more elegant.

Both horses and ponies are measured in 'hands' and inches – a hand is 4 inches (10cm). The maximum height for a pony and the minimum height for a horse is 14 hands and 2 inches. This is written 14.2hh ('hh' means 'hands high').

Horses and ponies can have all sorts of different coats. Some of them also have white patches or markings on their legs and faces.

Dappled

Chestnut, with a blaze

Palomino, with socks

Bay, with a star

Baby horses are called foals. After their first birthday, the females are known as fillies and the males as colts. Horses aren't ridden until they are about three years old. Fully grown male horses are either stallions or geldings. Stallions are used for breeding, while geldings make good riding horses. Female horses are called mares.

A family of wild horses

Famous breeds

There are hundreds of breeds of horses and ponies throughout the world. Each breed has different characteristics that have developed over many years.

Arab

People have been breeding Arabs for thousands of years. They are lively horses (as you can see from this picture of a stallion rearing) but they have a kind, gentle nature.

Thoroughbred

Thoroughbreds are the fastest horses in the world. Although they are bred for racing, a lot of competition horses are also part Thoroughbred.

Andalucian horses were first bred by monks - who had to hide their herds from plundering soldiers.

Andalucian

Although not very common today, these Spanish horses are still famed for their grace and beauty.

Appaloosa

Appaloosas have distinctive spotted coats. Underneath, they even have spotted skin.

In the past, Shetlands were prized pit ponies, used for work in mines, because of their small size.

Shetland

Shetlands are among the smallest ponies in the world, although they are very strong for their size.

Welsh Mountain Pony

Welsh Mountain Ponies are gentle, intelligent and sure-footed. These characteristics make them good riding ponies.

Shire

Shires are some of the biggest horses, and were bred for farming and pulling carts. They belong to a group of breeds known as heavy horses because of their strong build.

11

Horse talk

Horses are naturally friendly. In the wild they live in herds, so it's important that they can all get along. Even if they don't live in the wild, horses still enjoy company and are happy to treat people in the same way as they treat each other.

Just like people, horses can make friends. A horse might use his tail to swat flies away from his friend's face. Friends might also groom each other's coats with their lips and teeth.

When a horse is being groomed by someone he likes, he may try to groom them back by nibbling their shoulder.

Horses don't talk with words, as we do. Instead, they use body language.

When a horse is interested in something, he pricks his ears and holds his head and tail high.

An angry horse flattens his ears and bares his teeth. He may stamp his feet and swish his tail, too.

A happy, relaxed horse lets his head hang low. His ears flop out to the side and he may half-close his eyes.

Horse whispering

A horse whisperer is someone who understands and trains horses by using horses' natural instincts and body language. You can learn to understand horses too, by watching how they behave.

When a horse accepts someone as the leader of his herd, he will follow her lead.

Riding & pony care

Starting out

Learning to ride is about becoming part of a special team of two. A horse and rider can share everything from the thrill of jumping a tricky fence to the joy of racing through fields.

Most people learn to ride at a riding school. For riding, you should wear comfortable clothes, such as jeans or tracksuit bottoms, and sturdy shoes. You must also wear a hard hat to protect your head. Most riding schools can lend you a hat. If you ride a lot, you might want to buy your own hat and special riding clothes.

The boy on the left is wearing jeans and shoes with small heels. These clothes are fine to begin with.

This boy is wearing stretchy jodhpurs and boots specially designed for riding.

A pony has to wear a special outfit for riding, too. A saddle goes on his back, to make a seat for the rider. Sometimes the pony wears a saddlecloth or numnah underneath to make it more comfortable. A bridle buckles around the pony's head. The rider uses the bridle to guide the pony.

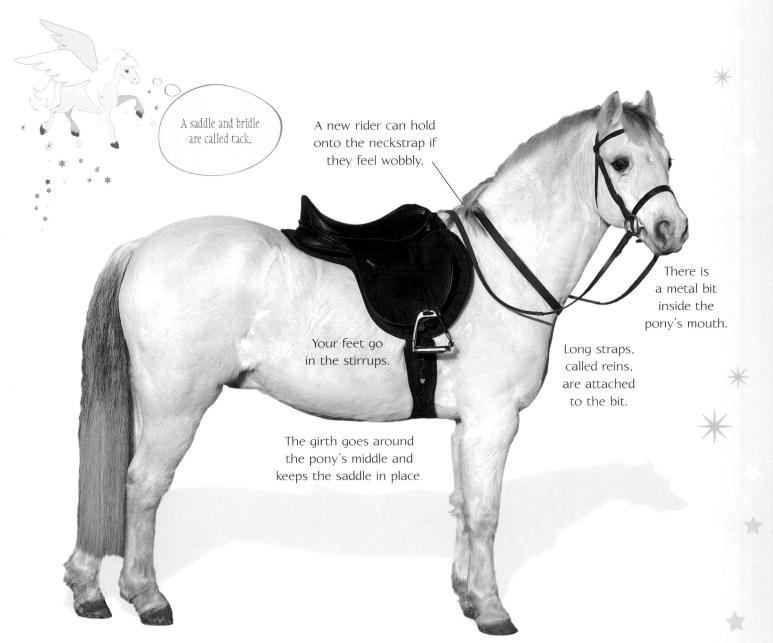

A saddle and bridle are called tack.

A new rider can hold onto the neckstrap if they feel wobbly.

There is a metal bit inside the pony's mouth.

Your feet go in the stirrups.

Long straps, called reins, are attached to the bit.

The girth goes around the pony's middle and keeps the saddle in place.

All aboard

Before your lesson, make friends with the pony you will be riding. Approach him from the side – if you walk behind him, he might be startled and kick. Say his name softly and hold your hand out flat, so the pony can sniff your fingers. Gently scratch his mane and neck.

You mount on the pony's left side. Put your left foot in the stirrup and hold the saddle firmly. Then push up with your other leg, and swing your bottom into the saddle.

Ask someone to help you mount the first few times.

When you dismount, take both feet out of the stirrups. Swing one leg over the pony's rump and lower yourself onto the ground.

18

Once you're on, sit up straight with your hands just above the front of the saddle. A rider with a good position will have their head, hips and heels in a straight line, with their toes pointing up a little.

Your position in the saddle is called your seat.

The reins go over your little fingers and come out under your thumbs. Your thumbs should be on the top, like in this picture. Hold the reins so that you can just feel the bit pressing lightly on the pony's mouth. Don't hold them too tightly, as this hurts the pony.

First steps

Lessons often take place in a fenced field, or an indoor or outdoor arena, called a school. One of the first things you will learn is how to walk around the school.

To get moving, nudge the pony's sides with both legs. Relax your hands so you don't pull on his mouth.

To turn left, gently squeeze your left hand on the reins. At the same time, put your left leg on the girth and move your right leg back a bit. (To turn right, you do the opposite.)

It helps to look in the direction you want to go.

To halt, sit deep in the saddle and pull back on the reins, gently but firmly.

There are lots of exercises that you can do to improve your balance. Ask someone to hold your pony's head while you do them.

Try leaning down and touching your right toe with your left hand. Then, touch your left toe with your right hand.

Try twisting both ways.

Stretch out your arms. Twist in the saddle so one arm points to the pony's head and one to his tail.

This exercise is called *Around the World*.

Take your feet out of the stirrups. Lift one leg over the pony's neck, then lift the other leg over his rump. Keep going until you are facing the right way again.

Moving on

Once you are comfortable walking, you are ready to trot. At trot, the pony moves his legs two at a time in a two-beat rhythm, which feels very bumpy.

There are two ways to ride when trotting. One is sitting trot, where you stay in the saddle. The other (shown above) is rising trot, where you rise out of the saddle every other beat.

Cantering is faster than trotting, but feels much smoother as the pony moves his legs in a gentle three-beat rhythm.

Galloping is faster than cantering and has a four-beat rhythm. It can be difficult to control a galloping horse, so only very experienced riders should try to do this.

New riders usually spend most of their time in a school, where there are fewer distractions for both pony and rider. But as your confidence grows and you become a better rider, you might want to try riding outside the school. This is known as hacking. Hacking along tracks and through fields is a fun way to see the countryside and improve your trotting and cantering.

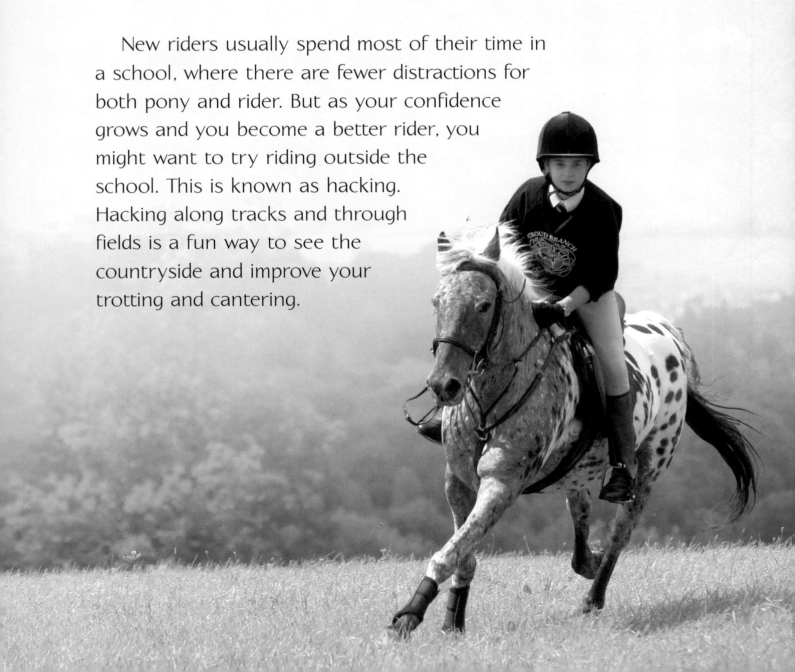

Jumping

From leaping over a log in a field to clearing a series of show fences, jumping can be exciting and rewarding. A pony and rider really have to work together to get everything right and clear a jump.

Jumping position

Before you start learning to jump, your instructor will probably ask you to shorten your stirrups. This helps you to move into the right position for jumping.

When a pony jumps, he stretches his neck and rounds his back. You can help him by leaning forward, so your bottom comes out of the saddle and your hands move closer to his ears. This is called the forward position.

24

Trotting poles

You can try out the forward position by trotting over poles on the ground. This improves your balance and encourages the pony to keep an even, bouncy stride.

Early jumps

When you feel confident trotting over poles, you can try small, simple jumps. A pole on the ground in front of the jump makes it easier for the pony to judge how high the jump is.

As the pony takes off, the rider moves into the forward position.

The pony rounds his back as he clears the jump.

On landing, the rider sits back and lets the reins slide through her fingers.

Helping hands

The more time you spend with ponies, the more you'll want to learn about taking care of them. A good way to start is by taking off the saddle and bridle after riding. This is called untacking. Ask someone to help you the first few times you do it.

Taking off the saddle

Slide both stirrups up their leather straps, then push the straps through the stirrups.

Lift the left saddleflap and undo the girth, then lower it under the pony's tummy.

Loop the girth over the other side of the saddle, then slide it off.

Taking off the bridle

Unbuckle the straps around the pony's nose and throat.

Use your right hand to lift the reins and the top of the bridle over his ears.

Rest your other hand on the pony's lips and slide the bit out of his mouth.

Horses and ponies need regular grooming, especially after riding, when they are hot and sweaty.

These ponies are wearing headcollars, so they can be tied up while being groomed.

Mud and dry sweat can be brushed off with a stiff dandy brush.

Use a soft body brush to brush the pony's coat, mane and tail.

A pony's hooves pick up dirt and stones. You can clean them using a hoofpick.

Hooves and shoes

Most riding horses wear metal shoes to stop their hooves from wearing down when they are ridden. Their shoes need changing about every six weeks by a farrier – someone who is specially trained in making and fitting horseshoes.

Keeping horses

In the wild, horses live outside all the time. It's best for riding horses to spend plenty of time in a field, too. Here they can graze, run around and enjoy being with other horses.

Horses love company, even if it's just a sheep!

Horses drink a lot, so the field must have a large trough of clean water in it. It's also good for there to be a shelter, where the horses can hide from flies in summer and bad weather in winter. If the weather is very cold, a horse can also wear a rug or blanket to keep him warm and dry.

A horse can also stay in a stable yard. Here, a horse relies on you for everything.

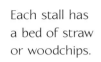
Each stall has a bed of straw or woodchips.

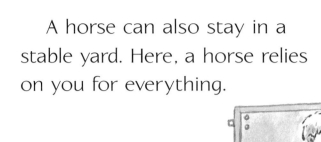

The stalls have to be 'mucked out' or cleaned every day.

Horses need plenty of water, and fresh hay to nibble.

If a horse is ridden a lot, he may need extra food, such as pony nuts, to give him more energy. Horses also like treats such as apples or carrots. Make sure you offer treats with your hand flat, so your fingers don't look like carrots too.

Even well-kept horses can get sick. Some illnesses, including coughs and colds, can be cured with good food and rest. But others such as colic, a kind of tummy ache, need treatment from a vet.

Competitions

Mounted games

Playing games on horseback can be a lot of fun – even if you're not an expert rider. Most games are really races testing speed and skills such as balance and aim. Riders can compete in races on their own or in teams, in mounted games competitions known as gymkhanas.

Bending

In a bending race, the pony and rider must weave in and out between a row of poles without knocking any over.

Flag race

A rider races to a tub full of flags, collects one and races back to their own tub. They keep racing back and forth until they have collected all the flags.

Prince Philip Cup

In 1957, Prince Philip of the United Kingdom started a competition designed to encourage teamwork, determination and enthusiasm among young riders. That year, mounted games teams competed for the very first Prince Philip Cup at the Horse of the Year Show in London, England.

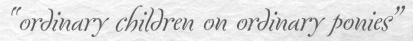

"ordinary children on ordinary ponies"

Prince Philip describing the Cup competitors

The event was a huge success and today, Pony Clubs in America, Canada and Australia run their own Prince Philip Cup competitions. Every year, teams across each country compete in regional heats. The winners go on to ride it out at national finals, to see who is the best of all.

Showing

Shows are like beauty contests for ponies. Like a true beauty queen, a star-quality show pony must have perfect features and good manners. Ponies are also judged on how smoothly they move around the show ring.

Riders wear elegant jackets and jodhpurs, and the ponies should have shiny coats and polished hooves. Some breeds are shown with natural flowing manes, but most ponies should have a plaited (braided) mane.

Preparing the mane

A small section is plaited (braided) and tied with thread.

Then, the section is rolled up and held in place with thread.

This is repeated along the mane to make a line of identical rolls.

There are lots of showing classes for horses and ponies of all shapes, sizes and breeds. Not all of these classes are ridden. Some ponies are shown 'in-hand' and are led around the ring instead.

Western shows

In America, some shows are ridden Western style – meaning the contestants use long stirrups and hold the reins with only one hand. The horses wear traditional Western tack and the riders wear cowboy hats and decorative boots and shirts.

Showjumping

Showjumping is tense and exciting – both for those taking part and for those who come to watch. Horses and riders jump a course of brightly painted fences under a strict time limit. Penalties, or faults, are given if they take too long, stop at a fence or knock one over.

The riders are allowed to walk around the course beforehand, to decide how to approach each jump. It's very important the rider knows exactly what to do, as the horse doesn't see the course first.

The higher and wider a fence, the more powerful the horse's jump needs to be.

Puissance

One of the most nerve-wracking competitions is the Puissance, where competitors try to clear a single wall. With each round the wall gets higher and higher, reaching heights of over 2m (7ft). Jumping this high requires great courage and absolutely perfect technique.

The bricks are very light so they don't hurt the horse if he knocks them.

Milton the superstar

Every horse is special to their rider, but Milton became special to thousands of showjumping fans. This handsome white horse was such a superstar, he even had his own fan club. Between 1985 and 1994, Milton and his rider, John Whitaker, won over a million pounds in prize money, setting a new record for showjumping.

Dressage

Horses move with natural elegance – but carrying a rider can change this. The goal of dressage is to create harmony between a horse and rider, so they move together with perfect grace and balance.

This horse is doing an extended trot, swinging each leg out as far as he can.

In a dressage competition, a horse and rider perform a series of moves in an arena. Each move is marked out of ten. The judges look to see that the horse is well-trained and listening to the rider's commands. It can take years for a horse and rider to master the most complex moves, especially at the highest level, known as Grand Prix.

The Spanish Riding School gets its name from the Spanish horses it once used.

The Spanish Riding School

Over two thousand years ago, the ancient Greeks used dressage to prepare their horses for battle. Today, these ancient battle moves can still be seen, performed to music, at the Spanish Riding School in Vienna. Because the moves are so demanding, the School uses only Lipizzaner horses, specially bred for their strength and intelligence, and popularly known as the dancing white horses of Vienna.

Traditional battle moves

Levade (a popular pose for statues)

Capriole

Courbette

Cross country

Cross country is a thrilling sport that tests speed, skill and courage. Jumps are set up across the countryside and competitors have to gallop long distances between them, within a set time limit.

Cross-country jumps are based on obstacles you might find out riding, such as banks, hedges and logs. Unlike showjumping fences, the jumps can't be knocked over. So riders wear back-protectors and horses wear boots to protect their legs.

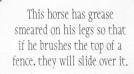

This horse has grease smeared on his legs so that if he brushes the top of a fence, they will slide over it.

Most courses include a water jump. Horses are naturally wary of water, so it takes patient training and a brave horse to tackle such a scary jump.

Eventing

Cross country is an important part of a three-day event – a competition which also covers dressage and showjumping. One of the most famous three-day events is held in the grounds of Badminton House in England. Badminton's cross-country course is one of the hardest in the world.

"Growing up, Badminton was the thing I most wanted to win."

Pippa Funnell MBE, a successful British event rider

Racing

A race starts and the horses spring into a gallop. Every one of them is trying to keep up with the herd, eager not to be left behind. This natural desire to race keeps wild horses safe from danger – and helps to make a champion racehorse.

Although every horse has the instinct to race, Thoroughbreds are the fastest of all. To help them go even faster, racehorses wear lightweight shoes and saddles. Even the jockeys who ride them try to be as light as possible.

The greatest racehorse?

Although every generation of racehorses has its star, in 1769 there was one who outshone them all. His name was Eclipse and he beat every horse he ever raced – by a long, long way. After winning 18 races he was forced to retire, because no one would let their horses run against him.

Eclipse (1770) by George Stubbs

"Eclipse first, the rest nowhere."

Captain Dennis O'Kelly, one of Eclipse's owners

Living on

When racehorses are very successful, they may be used for breeding. With any luck, their offspring will be as fast and brave as them and their success will live on.

Race jockeys wear bright shirts called silks.

Famous horses in
life and art

Fighting horses

Some of the most famous horses in history were the brave chargers who carried kings and warriors into battle – such as Bucephalus, the dark stallion tamed by Alexander the Great.

Coins celebrating fighting horses

At first, Bucephalus seemed impossible to ride. Men who tried were flung to the ground. Then Alexander mounted him and galloped into the sun. When he returned, he explained to the astonished onlookers that the horse had been afraid of his own shadow – which he couldn't see when facing the sun.

Inseparable

Alexander and Bucephalus went all over the world, and Bucephalus wouldn't be ridden by anyone else. When the horse eventually died in India, Alexander built him a grand tomb and founded a city named Bucephala in his memory.

This picture of Alexander and Bucephalus in battle is over 2,000 years old.

The white fool

Of all the horses in Spain, the finest were said to be the Andalucian herds kept by monks. One year, a monk gave young Rodrigo Diaz the pick of his herd. Rodrigo chose the weakest colt, making the monk exclaim "Babieca!" ("Fool!") Rodrigo gave this name to his horse – which grew up into a magnificent white charger.

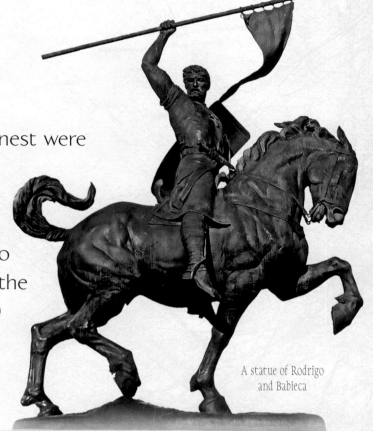

A statue of Rodrigo and Babieca

Rodrigo became a famous warrior, riding Babieca into all his battles. Together they were so successful, Rodrigo's enemies called him El Cid (My Lord). Rodrigo eventually died in battle, but faithful Babieca carried his body into one last fight. El Cid's enemies thought he had come back from the dead and fled, terrified. Babieca had won their last battle.

A monument in London dedicated to animals in war

Warhorses

Many ordinary horses have also served bravely in war, from cavalry horses who charged into combat to pack mules who carried soldiers' supplies.

Performing horses

A painting of a circus rosinback painted over a century ago

Rosinbacks

Horses' natural strength, grace and willingness to learn has made them a star feature of many shows. One traditional act involves horses known as rosinbacks, which canter patiently while their riders do acrobatic tricks. The horses' backs are sprinkled with rosin – a chalky powder – so the riders don't slip.

Liberty horses

Liberty horses perform without riders to guide them. They are trained to turn, stop, kneel or rear on command.

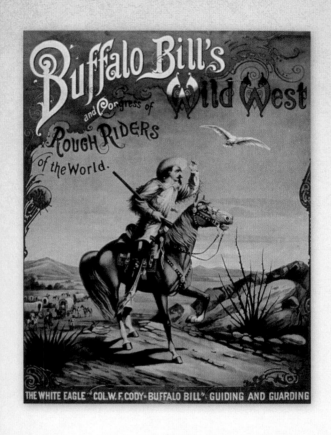

Wild West

One of the most successful shows ever was Buffalo Bill's Wild West Show. Buffalo Bill started out riding and hunting buffalo on the American frontier. Then he formed a group of "Rough Riders" who put on shows filled with dramatic stunts – such as holding up a stagecoach or leaping between galloping horses. They were so popular, they toured the world for 30 years and performed for Queen Victoria.

Dancing stallion

One of the most spectacular performances of recent times was given by a white Lipizzaner stallion, which appeared in the opera *Carmen*. While the leading lady sang a famous song about love, the stallion danced with her, stepping gracefully in time to the music.

Working horses

For centuries before cars
and trucks, horsepower
ruled. Nearly everyone
rode, or used horse-drawn
carts and carriages.
In towns, horses pulled
the buses and trams. On
farms, they worked in the
fields and carried in the
harvest. And in deep underground mines,
sturdy pit ponies hauled heavy loads of coal.

An old horse bus

Even today, there are many working horses around the
world. Some are trained for shows and festivals. But others
are just ordinary horses, working on farms, pulling
carts and carrying riders, as their
ancestors used to do.

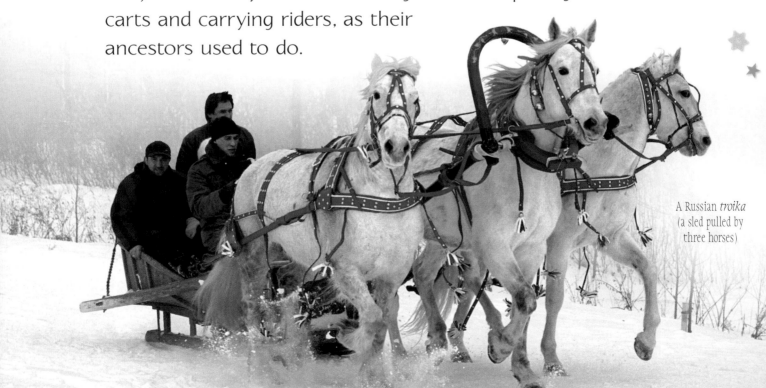

A Russian *troika*
(a sled pulled by
three horses)

Pony Express

In America, the first fast postal service relied on horses and was named the Pony Express. Teams of dedicated horses and riders delivered letters in relays, crossing the continent in just ten days. In the days before telephones, this was by far the fastest way to send news.

Police horses

Many police forces use specially trained horses. Probably the most famous are the Royal Canadian Mounted Police – known as the Mounties. They were founded over a hundred years ago, to patrol remote areas of Canada. Today, handpicked teams of Mounties still dazzle audiences with dramatic shows of horsemanship.

The Mounties always ride specially bred black horses.

Storybook stars

National Velvet

Velvet Brown is just an ordinary girl
who dreams of owning a horse.
Then, amazingly, she wins one in a
raffle – a talented but unruly racehorse
named Pie. *National Velvet* was written by Enid Bagnold,
who probably based Pie on one of her own horses.

National Velvet was
made into a film starring
horse-loving actress Liz Taylor.

Black Beauty

Black Beauty is the star of a
story by horse-lover Anna Sewell.
Anna lived in Victorian England
and saw how cruelly some
working horses were treated. She
wrote *Black Beauty* to show life
from a horse's point of view.
Her book was a huge hit, and
helped people to understand
and treat horses better.

Black Beauty has been
filmed many times.
This photo is from a
1994 version.

*"they do not suffer less
because they have no words"*

Anna Sewell, writing about horses

Misty of Chincoteague

On a tiny, windswept island off the eastern coast of America, wild ponies roam free. But once a year, the residents of nearby Chincoteague round up the ponies for a horse sale. Misty was one such pony. Author Marguerite Henry fell in love with Misty on a visit to Chincoteague, bought her and wrote her story.

Misty and Marguerite

My Friend Flicka

Flicka is a fine chestnut filly, one of many horses on an American ranch. The ranch owner believes she is too wild to train – but his son Ken is determined to prove him wrong. Writer Mary O'Hara based the story on her experience of ranch life.

The Silver Brumby

Deep in the Australian outback live herds of wild horses known as brumbies. This book by Elyne Mitchell tells the adventures of a silver brumby stallion named Thowra. Elyne, an eager rider from childhood, wrote the story for her children.

53

Mythical horses

Over the centuries, many myths and legends have sprung up about horses. Three of the most famous are described here – and you will find more horse myths retold in the next section.

Sea horses

The ancient Romans worshipped Neptune as the God of the Sea and Horses. According to myth, Neptune rode in a chariot pulled by sea horses. In rough seas, the Romans said you could see the horses' manes appearing as white crests on the waves.

Neptune's Horses (1910) by Walter Crane

Unicorns

Long ago, hunters searched desperately for magical, horse-like unicorns. According to myth, it was almost impossible to catch a unicorn. But if a virtuous maiden sat and waited, the unicorn would come and lay its head in her lap.

The unicorn's precious spiral horn was supposed to cure any poison and was worth its weight in gold. In fact, the horns treasured by many kings and queens really came from a kind of whale known as the Narwhal.

Chalk horse

The White Horse of Uffington is around 3,000 years old. It was cut into the chalk of an English hillside by an ancient Celtic tribe, and probably represents a horse goddess. On moonlit nights, locals say it climbs down and goes to feed in a nearby valley known as The Manger.

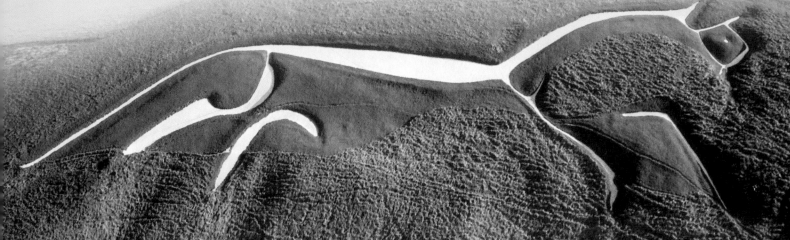

Horses in art

Artists have always been
inspired by horses' natural
beauty. This page shows some
of the best-known horses in art
– and the rest of this section reveals how
to create fantastic horse pictures of your own.

This bronze horse
was made about 2,000
years ago in China.

Whistlejacket

One of the most famous horse artists of all was George
Stubbs. An expert on horses, he even published a book
on horse anatomy. This painting
shows the champion racehorse,
Whistlejacket. George lovingly
captured every detail of the
horse's powerful body.

George painted this
picture of Whistlejacket
in about 1762.

Horse sketches

These horses were drawn by enthusiastic rider and artist Theodore Gericault. Theodore was passionate about horses, cramming his notebooks with sketches. Sadly, he died young after falling off a horse.

Thelwell ponies

Norman Thelwell made his name drawing pony cartoons. He had a great hit with scenes of mischievous but sweet Shetland ponies.

Horsey feelings

German artist Franz Marc admired horses' noble nature and spirit. He made dozens of paintings to try to express his feelings,, creating bright, striking pictures like this blue horse.

Drawing horses and foals

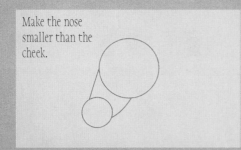

1. Draw two circles for a horse's cheek and nose. Add curved lines between the two circles.

2. Add ears on top of the head. Draw a big bean shape for the body, then add lines for the neck.

3. Draw the legs, making one front leg bend a little. Add lines near the bottom of each leg, for the hooves.

4. Draw the horse's mane and tail. Add a forelock between the ears, then draw the eyes and mouth.

5. Draw tiny circles for a foal's cheek and nose. Draw a short bean-shaped body, then add the neck.

6. Draw legs that are the same length as the horse's legs, but a little thinner. Add a face, mane and tail.

7. Draw around the horse and foal using a brown pencil. Then, erase all the other pencil lines.

You could use pencils if you don't have any chalk.

8. Fill in the horse and the foal using different shades of chalk or chalk pastel. Add grass and sky, too.

Magical horse painting

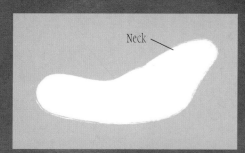

Neck

1. Dip your finger in white paint. Finger paint a bean shape for the horse's body and a curve for the neck.

2. Add a circle and a shape for the nose on top of the neck. Then, use your little finger to add dots for ears.

3. Finger paint the legs and add a shape for a wing. Then, print lots of feathers with your finger.

This background was painted before the horse, then the clouds were added using chalks.

You could fingerprint silver spots on the body, too.

4. Dip a paintbrush in silver paint, then paint the horse's hooves, mane and tail. Leave the paint to dry.

5. Add a face using pencils. Then, decorate the horse's mane, tail and legs using a gold pen.

6. For a magical trail, brush white glue around the horse. Sprinkle glitter over the glue and add sequins.

Myths and stories

Some of the stories contain tricky names. You can find out how to say them on page 95.

The winged horse

Prince Bellerophon was in trouble. A terrible monster, the Chimaera, was attacking the Kingdom of Lycia, where he was staying. The Chimaera had the heads of a lion and a goat, and the tail of a serpent. When it opened its mouth, it breathed out deadly flames. And the King of Lycia wanted Bellerophon to fight it!

Bellerophon was a bold rider and a brave fighter, and he loved adventure. Even so, he hesitated to agree... until he caught the eye of Princess Philonoe, the King's beautiful daughter. "I'll do it," he blurted. Philonoe smiled shyly. "Good luck," she whispered, hiding her blushes behind a curtain of dark hair.

Brave as Bellerophon was, he knew he could not defeat the monster without help. So he went to see a wise man. "How can I fight the Chimaera?" he asked. "You will need a lead-tipped spear

and a winged horse," replied the wise man. And he told Bellerophon about Pegasus, a wild, white stallion with huge, white-feathered wings sprouting from his shoulders. Pegasus, he told the astonished prince, could fly through the air as easily as other horses walked along the ground.

"I have plenty of weapons... but how will I find this wonderful horse?" asked Bellerophon.

"That won't be easy," the wise man admitted. "No one has ever tamed Pegasus. He lives high in the mountains, out of man's reach. You will need the help of the gods to catch him." And he told Bellerophon to pray to the goddess Athena.

Bellerophon went to Athena's temple and prayed all night. Eventually, he fell asleep – and dreamed he saw Athena, dressed in dazzling white and gold. In one hand, she grasped a shining golden bridle which she held out to Bellerophon.

"This is my gift to you," she said. "Find the mountain spring where Pegasus goes to drink. If you catch him before he flies away, this bridle will tame him."

When Bellerophon awoke, he was still clutching the bridle. "It's real!" he exclaimed. "Now I must find the spring." He set out at once for the mountains, pausing only to fetch a spear and his bow and arrows.

Bellerophon searched until he found a remote spring with hoofprints by the water's edge. "This must be the spot," he decided, hiding nearby. Sure enough, before long he heard a rush of wings. It was Pegasus. The winged horse landed by the water, shook his mane and lowered his head to drink.

The prince sprang up and threw the bridle over the horse's head. Pegasus snorted and splashed and spread his wings, but Bellerophon held on tight. As he buckled the last strap, Pegasus grew quiet.

Gently, Bellerophon
stroked the horse's proudly
arched neck. Pegasus stood
patiently as Bellerophon picked up
his weapons and vaulted onto his
back. Then, with a shake of the reins,
they soared into the sky.

Bellerophon gasped as the landscape
unfurled. Toy-sized trees, fields and villages
spread out below. Far off, he could see black
smoke. "The Chimaera," he muttered, urging
Pegasus on.

As they flew closer, Bellerophon saw
burned houses and abandoned farms. The
Chimaera crouched in the middle of a
blackened wasteland. When it saw the
flying horse, it snarled and unleashed
a jet of flame – but it couldn't reach
as high as Pegasus.

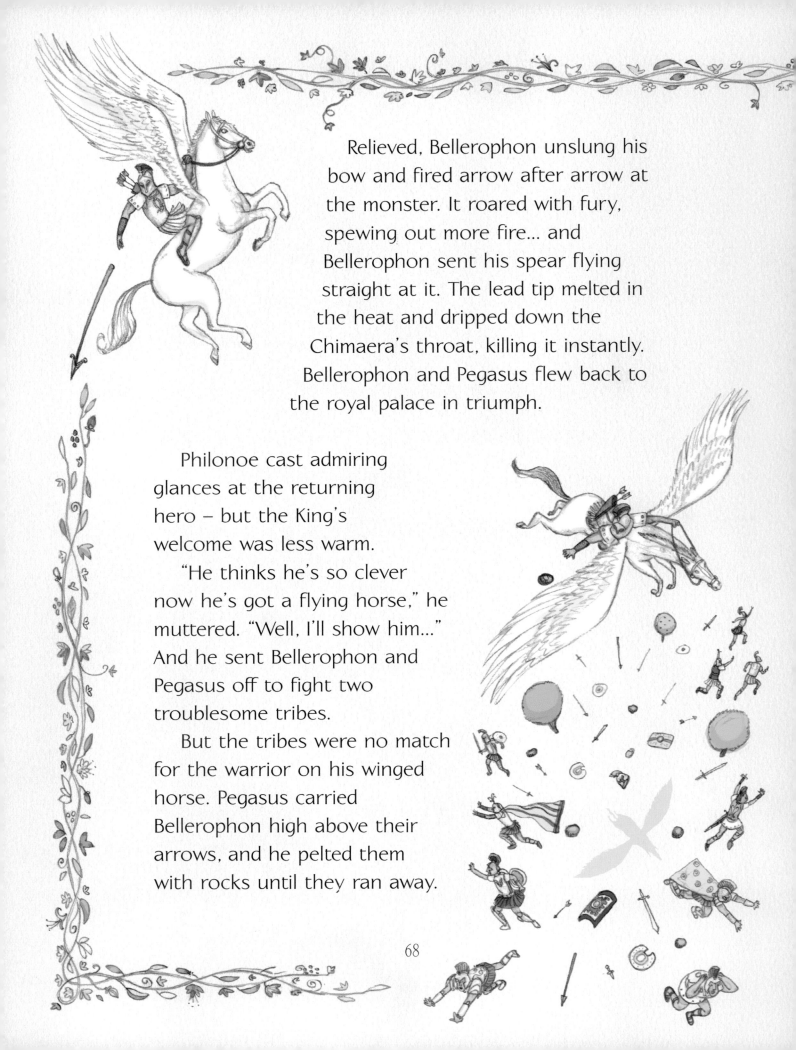

Relieved, Bellerophon unslung his bow and fired arrow after arrow at the monster. It roared with fury, spewing out more fire... and Bellerophon sent his spear flying straight at it. The lead tip melted in the heat and dripped down the Chimaera's throat, killing it instantly. Bellerophon and Pegasus flew back to the royal palace in triumph.

Philonoe cast admiring glances at the returning hero – but the King's welcome was less warm.

"He thinks he's so clever now he's got a flying horse," he muttered. "Well, I'll show him..." And he sent Bellerophon and Pegasus off to fight two troublesome tribes.

But the tribes were no match for the warrior on his winged horse. Pegasus carried Bellerophon high above their arrows, and he pelted them with rocks until they ran away.

Next, Bellerophon and Pegasus sank a pirate ship
and crushed a group of rogue soldiers. Finally, even the
King realized they could not be defeated. "This young
man must be blessed by the gods," he told himself –
and decided to offer Bellerophon his daughter's hand
in marriage.

So one fine summer day, Bellerophon and the
beautiful Philonoe were married, to a joyous ringing
of bells. And the wedding procession was led by a
wonderful winged horse wearing a shining golden bridle.

The horses of the sun

Each day, four fiery horses pulled Helios's golden chariot across the sky. Their journey began at dawn and ended at dusk, for Helios was the sun god, who brought light and warmth to the world.

There were eight sun-horses in all, named Firebright, Flame, Fleetfoot, Thunder, Scarlet, Scorcher, Blaze and Shine. They were wild, powerful animals with blazing chestnut coats. Their breath was hot with flames and their golden hooves struck showers of burning sparks at every step. It took all of Helios's strength and skill to keep them on the right path.

Helios lived in a glittering golden palace, where glowing ivory columns held up a roof sparkling with precious stones. The stones were arranged like the stars of the heavens, showing the constellations that he passed each day on his journey.

Apart from the company of his horses, Helios led a lonely life. He had once loved the sea nymph Clymene, but she lived far away on Earth with their son, Phaeton.

Helios looked down on the boy each day, as his chariot swept through the skies, but Phaeton never saw him – only the sunlight he brought. Still, Phaeton longed to meet his father and begged his mother to tell him how to find him.

Eventually, his mother gave in. "Walk east, into the sunrise," she told him, "until you see a golden palace. That is where your father lives."

So Phaeton set out and, after walking for a day and a night, found himself in a meadow of sweet-smelling herbs, grazed by eight magnificent chestnut horses. He paused to admire them.

71

Then, through the pre-dawn mist, Phaeton saw a shimmering golden palace, just as his mother had described. Taking a deep breath, he mounted the steep steps that led to the entrance.

Inside, Helios sat on a diamond throne. His crown of sunrays shone so brightly Phaeton had to shield his eyes from the glare. As soon as Helios saw him, he threw off the crown and wrapped the boy in a hug.

"So it's true. You are my father," whispered Phaeton.

"Yes," replied Helios with a broad smile. "And to prove it, I will grant any wish you have. I swear it by the heavens! I am so happy to see you."

Phaeton already knew what he wanted. "Were those your horses outside?" he asked. "Please, let me drive them! I've always wanted to race horses like those – and when people see me in your chariot, they will know I really am a god's son."

Helios frowned. "Ask for something else," he pleaded. "Only I should drive the sun chariot. The road across the sky is narrow, and my horses are wild and strong. I am afraid you could not control them."

But Phaeton would not be deterred, and Helios could not break his vow. With a heavy heart, he harnessed the horses. As dawn approached, Phaeton climbed eagerly into the chariot. Gently, Helios wiped a magic cream over the boy's face, to protect him from the heat, and set the sunray crown on his head.

"Hold the reins tightly and follow the wheel tracks between the stars," he instructed. "And don't let the horses run off with you! If you go too high, the world below will freeze – too low, and it will catch fire."

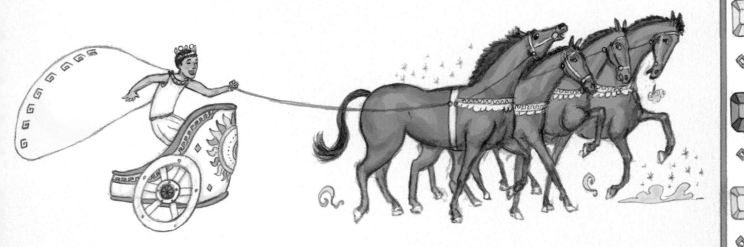

Phaeton nodded, impatient to be off. He barely heard his father. As soon as Helios had finished, he shook the reins and the fiery horses leaped forward. "Whoopee!" he shouted happily, feeling their power.

"Take care," cried Helios behind him, but his words were lost in the wind.

Snorting flames, the chestnut horses dashed up into the dawn sky. The chariot, with only a boy's weight to steady it, bounced violently from side to side. Startled, the horses veered sideways. Phaeton hauled on the reins, but the horses were stronger. Soon they were off the road and among the stars, which began to sizzle and smoke in the unaccustomed heat.

Phaeton glanced down, searching for the wheel tracks, but saw only miles of empty darkness. The world was far, far below. He reeled, overcome with dizziness, and the reins slipped from his fingers.

Given their freedom, the horses dashed headlong through the clouds, which began to burn up, then plunged down, scorching the earth. Trees burst into flames and oceans steamed. Mountain tops melted and rooves cracked. The world was catching fire, filling the air with burning smoke.

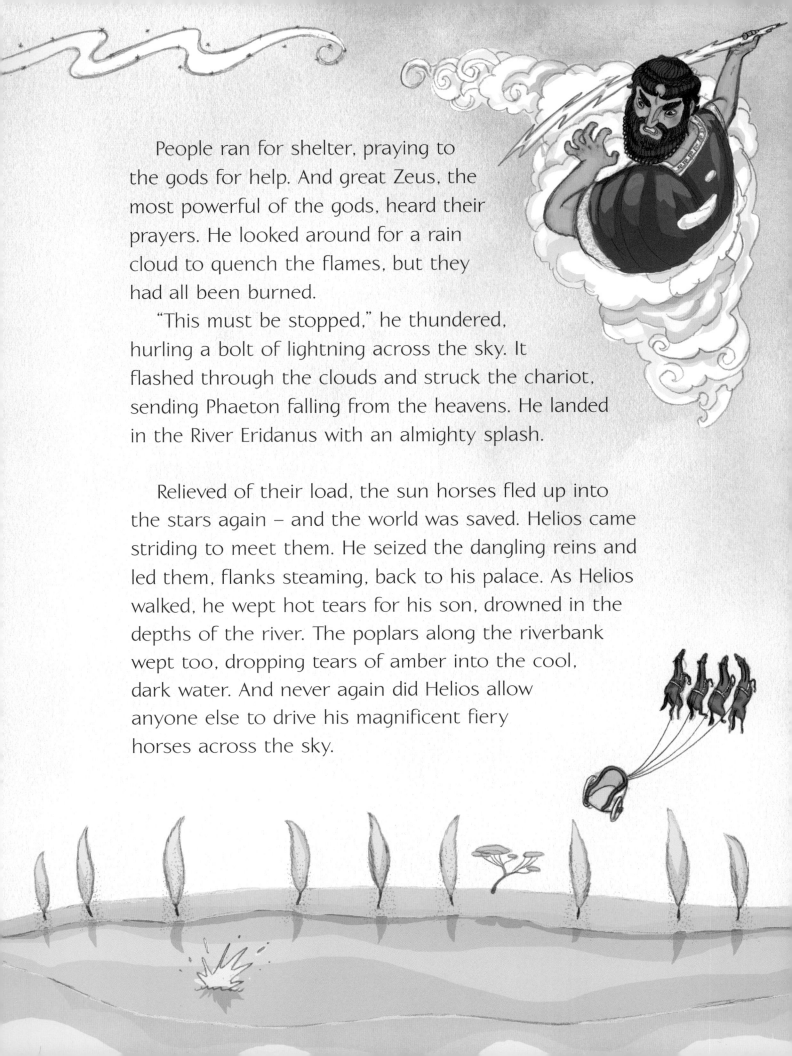

People ran for shelter, praying to the gods for help. And great Zeus, the most powerful of the gods, heard their prayers. He looked around for a rain cloud to quench the flames, but they had all been burned.

"This must be stopped," he thundered, hurling a bolt of lightning across the sky. It flashed through the clouds and struck the chariot, sending Phaeton falling from the heavens. He landed in the River Eridanus with an almighty splash.

Relieved of their load, the sun horses fled up into the stars again – and the world was saved. Helios came striding to meet them. He seized the dangling reins and led them, flanks steaming, back to his palace. As Helios walked, he wept hot tears for his son, drowned in the depths of the river. The poplars along the riverbank wept too, dropping tears of amber into the cool, dark water. And never again did Helios allow anyone else to drive his magnificent fiery horses across the sky.

Sleipner and Goldfax

One-eyed Odin, the father of the gods, was fiercely proud of his horse, Sleipner – and with good reason. Sleipner was no ordinary horse. He was a magnificent silver stallion with eight legs, who could race across the seas, through the skies or over solid ground with equal ease.

One spring morning, Odin saddled Sleipner beneath the great ash tree, which spread its branches over Asgard, the home of the gods. Then he rode out in search of adventure.

Sleipner danced with energy. Odin laughed to feel the horse's eagerness and spurred him on. They skimmed over the ocean which surrounded Asgard, scattering diamond-bright drops of spray.

As a wall of mountains loomed ahead, Sleipner rose into the sky, treading silently on thin air. Warily, Odin surveyed the stony landscape below. This was the land of the giants – ancient enemies of the gods. Long ago, Odin had slain the oldest giant, a cruel, ice-hearted monster, and the gods and giants had been at war ever since.

Among the rocks, a flash of gold caught Odin's eye. He twitched the reins to bring Sleipner down for a closer look... and saw a magnificent horse, its coat gleaming in the sun like spun gold.

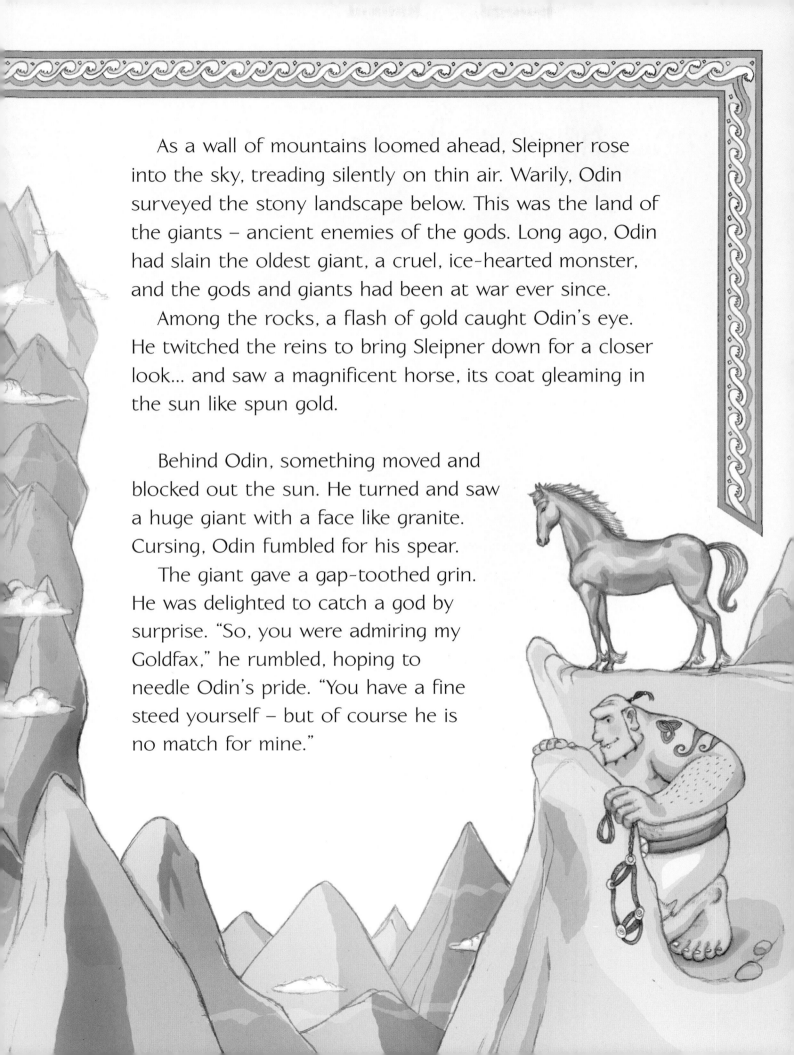

Behind Odin, something moved and blocked out the sun. He turned and saw a huge giant with a face like granite. Cursing, Odin fumbled for his spear.

The giant gave a gap-toothed grin. He was delighted to catch a god by surprise. "So, you were admiring my Goldfax," he rumbled, hoping to needle Odin's pride. "You have a fine steed yourself – but of course he is no match for mine."

Odin frowned. "Your horse may be pretty," he replied crossly, "but mine is faster..."

"Prove it," chuckled the giant, with a sound like falling boulders.

"Very well," snapped Odin. "Let's race. Ready?"

The giant sprang onto his horse. "Ready!" he boomed. And they were off, a silver streak and a golden one, disappearing into the distance.

Now there was no sound but rushing wind and thudding hooves. Flecks of foam spattered the horses' outstretched necks as they chased each other across the grassy plains of the world and beyond.

Odin was determined not to be beaten by a giant. He urged Sleipner on until the horse's eight legs were a blur. Gradually, the silver stallion pulled in front. Before long, the rainbow bridge which led to Asgard loomed ahead. The riders dashed straight over it without pausing, only pulling up when they reached the ash tree.

Sleipner had won. The other gods gathered around, cheering Odin and slapping the stallion's heaving flanks. Only now did the giant realize where he was – in Asgard, surrounded by his deadliest enemies. He looked around nervously. "Maybe the race was a trap," he thought, with a shiver.

But Odin turned and gave him a broad, welcoming smile. The thrill of the race had put old grudges out of his head. "This giant raced bravely," he announced. "Tonight, he is our guest."

That evening, the halls of Asgard rang with music and merriment as a great feast was served. For a few hours, the gods and the giant forgot their differences and ate and drank together. And in the stables, Sleipner and Goldfax whinnied softly to each other as they shared their hay.

Rakush

Among the mountains of ancient Persia, where the sun burned in summer and blizzards howled in winter, lived herds of wild horses. They were fine animals, as fast as the wind and as tough as the rocky landscape in which they lived. And finest of them all was a young colt named Rakush.

Rakush had a beautiful red-brown coat, with golden dapples. Beneath his skin, his muscles rippled like a lion's. He was so swift, he could easily outrun all the other horses – which is what had earned him the name Rakush, meaning lightning.

The men of the mountains longed to capture Rakush, but the colt's mother defended him fiercely. If any man came near them, she would kick and bite until he fled.

The mountain lands were ruled by Zal,
whose son, Rustam, was a promising warrior.
One summer, Rustam begged his father for a
steed of his own. So Zal ordered a huge gathering of
horses. "Everyone must bring their finest horses to my
palace, on pain of death," he commanded. "My son will
choose one, and I will fill the hands of the man who
brings it with gold."

On the appointed day, the plain before Zal's palace was
crowded with horses of every description. All the horse
dealers and horse lords had brought their best animals,
and the men of the mountains had driven down the
wild herds. Rakush and his mother had come too,
reluctant to be left behind, but they were as wild
and unapproachable as ever.

One by one, the horses were led before Zal
and Rustam. And one by one, Rustam tested
their strength by laying his hand heavily
on their shoulder. But each horse
trembled under the pressure.

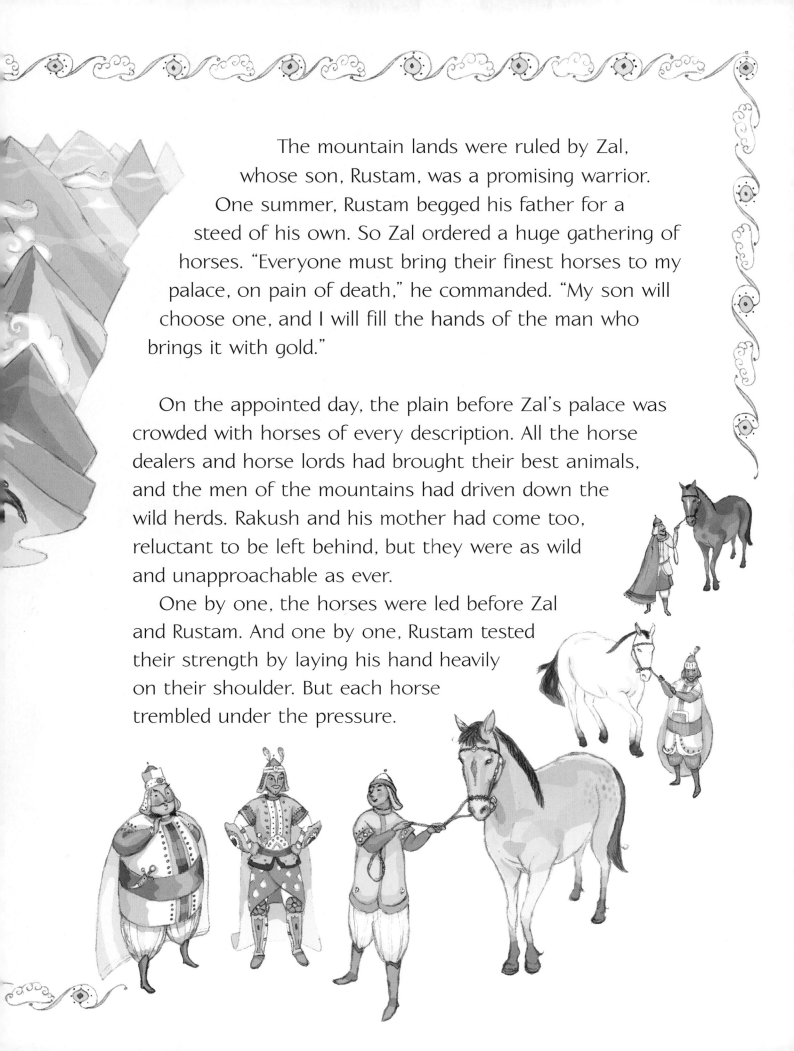

"I must have a horse as strong as me," Rustam sighed, looking across the horse-filled plain. Suddenly, his eye lighted on a magnificent red-brown colt. "What horse is that?" he demanded. "Bring him to me."

To his surprise, no one claimed the colt. Instead, one of the mountain men bowed apologetically. "We call him Rakush," he said. "No one can tame him or his mother – for three years we have tried to catch him and failed. Please, my lord, choose another horse."

But Rustam had made up his mind. He picked up a halter and walked over to Rakush. The colt's mother snorted dangerously and bared her teeth – but Rustam looked her in the eye and spoke, and she fell quiet.

Now Rustam caught Rakush and tried his strength, and the colt stood firm. Then the warrior swung up onto the colt's back and galloped off across the plain. And to everyone watching, it was clear – this horse and rider were made for each other.

From then on, Rustam and Rakush were inseparable. Whenever Rustam was sent to fight the enemies of Persia, Rakush bore him eagerly.

One day, Rustam was summoned to the aid of a distant king. Rakush covered the miles so fast that, by nightfall, they were deep in the wilderness. Rustam was soon snoring, not realizing a lion lurked nearby. But Rakush could smell the lion and did not sleep.

The lion watched hungrily. It crept closer, then suddenly pounced – but Rakush was waiting. He lashed out with his hooves and the lion fell to the ground, dead. Now Rustam woke. Instead of praising his horse, he frowned. "You should not fight on your own," he grumbled. "Suppose you'd been killed, how could I have continued my journey?" Rakush hung his head.

The next day, Rakush and Rustam had a long, tiring journey across a burning desert. As the sun sank, they found a leafy oasis where they decided to rest. Before going to sleep, Rustam warned his horse – "If an enemy comes tonight, wake me. Do not fight alone!"

Now, this oasis was the home of a poisonous dragon. After dark, it came slithering out of its hole – and Rakush obediently stamped and neighed to wake his master. The noise made the dragon slip back, so that when Rustam looked, there was nothing to be seen. "Silly horse, you have woken me for nothing," he grumbled, settling back under his cloak.

As soon as Rustam began to snore, the dragon crept out again. Again, Rakush woke Rustam – and again the dragon hid itself. This time, Rustam was angry. "Why won't you let me sleep?" he shouted, pulling his cloak over himself once more. Rakush pawed the ground in frustration.

When the dragon appeared for the third time, Rakush hesitated, then gave a loud neigh. Rustam sprang to his feet, furious to be woken again – and saw the dragon sliding silently in his direction.

Rustam pulled out his sword. Before he could strike, the dragon coiled itself around him and squeezed. Rustam's arms were pinned to his sides and he could hardly breathe. "I'm done for!" he gasped. But Rakush had other ideas. He darted forward, sank his teeth into the dragon and pulled, until his master was free again. Immediately, Rustam plunged his sword into the monster.

With the dragon dead at his feet, Rustam turned to his horse. "I am sorry I doubted you," he cried, flinging his arms around the horse's neck. "I owe you my life, noble friend."

Rakush pushed his nose against Rustam's shoulder and whinnied his forgiveness. And from that day forth, through all their adventures, nothing ever divided the two friends again.

The good-luck horse

In the far north of China lived a poor farmer and his son, Lee. They spent their days working in stony fields in the shadow of the Great Wall – an immense barrier which protected China from the wilds of Mongolia. Farming was back-breaking work, but one thing made life easier for them and that was their horse, Jing.

Jing was a stocky black stallion who could till the hard ground as easily as if it were soft butter. And when he carried water from the well, you would think the heavy cans were filled with nothing but air.

Each morning, Lee fetched Jing from the pasture and led him up to the farm to work. And each evening, Lee rubbed him down and turned him out again, to kick up his heels and gallop through the grass.

One bright spring morning, Lee went to fetch Jing as usual – but the stallion was nowhere to be seen. After searching everywhere, Lee ran to find his father.

"Jing's gone!" he wailed. "He must have found a way past the Wall. We'll never get him back now. How will we work the fields? It's such bad luck."

But the old farmer just smiled. "Maybe, maybe not," he told his son. "Maybe some good will come of this. Who knows?"

A few months later, Lee was weeding the fields when he heard hooves. Looking up, he saw Jing, whinnying happily, followed by a beautiful cream mare with a dark mane and tail. The stallion had come home again, and he had brought a mate – a wild mare from the Mongolian plains. Delighted, Lee ran to tell his father.

"You'll never believe our luck," Lee cried happily. "Jing is back – and he's brought a mare with him. What good fortune!"

To his surprise, his father frowned. "Maybe, maybe not," he replied. "Who knows how this will turn out?"

Lee was too happy to notice his father's caution. He had already named the mare Fu, which means good luck in Chinese.

He gazed at her admiringly. "She's a fine beast," he muttered, running one hand over her flanks. "I wonder what she's like to ride?" Impatient to find out, he leaped onto her back.

"Careful!" warned his father – but it was too late. The mare had never been ridden before and began to buck wildly, desperate to shake off the unaccustomed weight. Lee clutched at her tossing mane, but the silken strands slipped through his fingers and he fell heavily to the ground, with his leg twisted under him.

"Aaargh!" screamed Lee. "I think I've broken my leg. I wish I'd never set eyes on that mare, she's bad luck."

"Maybe, maybe not," replied his father. "Let's see how things turn out." And he helped his son to hobble home and bind his leg.

In time, Lee's leg healed – but crooked, so he walked with a limp. But whenever he grumbled, his father would stop him, saying, "Wait and see! You never know what will happen next."

And indeed, no one knew that Mongolian warriors were about to storm the Great Wall and attack China. The battle, when it came, was fierce and many men died. Desperate to replace them, the Chinese generals recruited young men from all the farms and villages along the Wall. But they didn't take Lee. "You can't fight with a leg like that," they told him.

Lee breathed a sigh of relief. He had been spared – thanks to Fu. "You're right," he told his father, "you just never know!"

The old horse of Atri

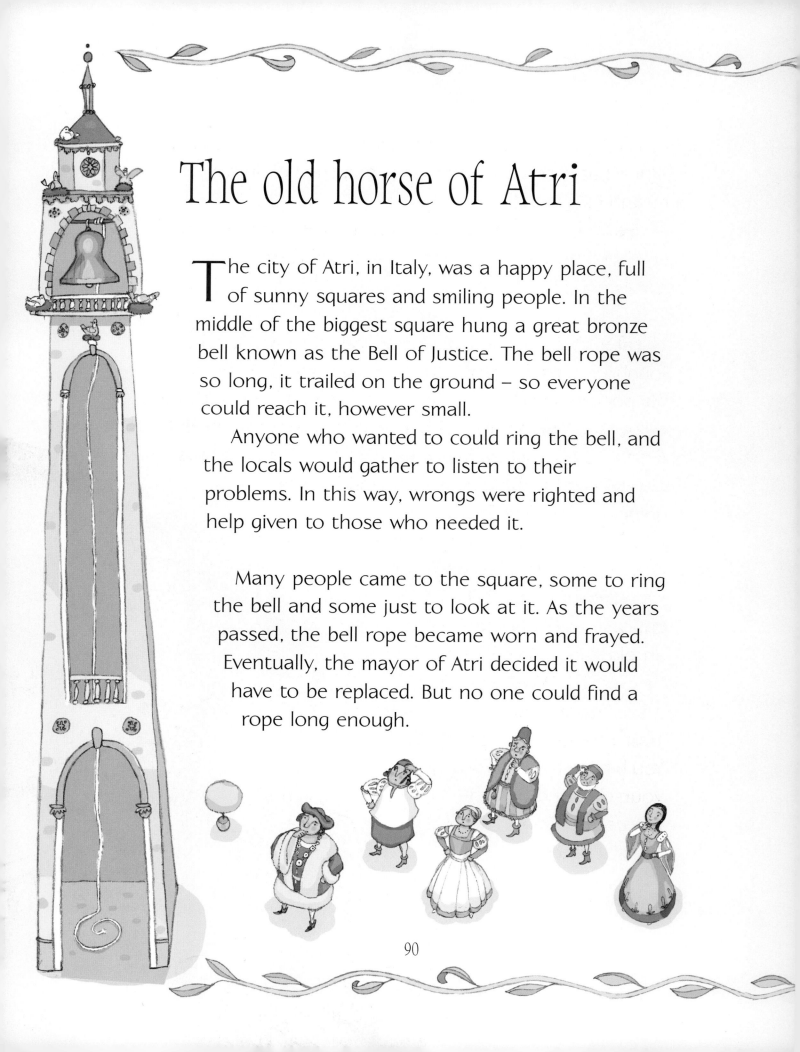

The city of Atri, in Italy, was a happy place, full of sunny squares and smiling people. In the middle of the biggest square hung a great bronze bell known as the Bell of Justice. The bell rope was so long, it trailed on the ground – so everyone could reach it, however small.

Anyone who wanted to could ring the bell, and the locals would gather to listen to their problems. In this way, wrongs were righted and help given to those who needed it.

Many people came to the square, some to ring the bell and some just to look at it. As the years passed, the bell rope became worn and frayed. Eventually, the mayor of Atri decided it would have to be replaced. But no one could find a rope long enough.

"We'll have to get a rope made specially," he sighed. "But what if someone needs to ring the bell in the meantime?"

"I know," said the deputy mayor. "We can use a vine!" So they cut a long, green vine and tied it to the bell, leaves and all.

Later that day, an old soldier rode into Atri. He had fought successfully in many wars and was coming home, his pockets lined with gold. His horse had been with him through every battle and had once been a magnificent beast – but now the horse was old too. His back was hollow and his mane was thin, and he was going lame in one foot.

Outside his house, the soldier dismounted. He lifted down his saddle bags, then looked critically at his horse. "What an old nag you've become," he mocked. "Well, you're no use to me now, and your food is too expensive. You'll have to fend for yourself!" And he sent the poor animal limping away.

The old horse was very hungry, but he couldn't see any grass – only neat stone houses and cobbled streets. One house had flowers growing outside, but when he bent his head to take a bite, an angry housewife chased him away.

Eventually, the horse found himself in a large, open square with a tower in the middle. And dangling from the tower was a leafy green vine. So he limped across to the tower and seized a mouthful of leaves.

"Ding-dong!" went the bell. And again, "Ding-dong!" The hungry old horse kept pulling at the leaves, the bell kept ringing – and the people of Atri came running to see who was calling for help.

"It's a horse!" exclaimed the mayor in astonishment. "And look how thin he is. Who does he belong to?"

There was a scuffle at the back of the crowd and then the old soldier was pushed forward.

"He was mine, but I turned him loose," he admitted. "I can't afford to feed him any more."

"That's not true," someone shouted. "His pockets are full of gold."

"Are they?" said the mayor. "Turn out your pockets!"

Reluctantly, the soldier reached into his pocket and brought out a handful of coins.

"You have plenty of money," snapped the mayor. "I order you to spend it on your horse. Build him a comfortable stall, feed him the finest oats and make sure he spends his old age in comfort."

As the crowd cheered, the soldier hung his head in shame. To tell the truth, he had already started to miss his former companion.

"What you ask is no more than my old friend deserves," he admitted, leading his horse away. And horse and master lived out their old age together in luxury.

Horsey words

Body brush – A soft brush used to get dust and grease out of a horse's coat.

Coat – The short hair all over a horse's body.

Colt – A young male horse (between one and four years old).

Cross country – A sport where competitors race through countryside to complete a series of jumps.

Dandy brush – A stiff brush used to get dry mud out of a horse's coat.

Dismounting – Getting off a horse.

Dressage – A sport where horses and riders perform set moves designed to test the harmony between them.

Farrier – Someone who cares for a horse's hooves and fits him with shoes.

Faults – Penalties given for mistakes in riding competitions.

Filly – A young female horse (between one and four years old).

Foal – A horse less than one year old.

Forelock – The part of the mane which falls between a horse's ears.

Forward position – How a rider sits for jumping, leaning forward to take the weight off the horse's back.

Gelding – A male horse or pony, generally used for riding.

Grooming – Cleaning a horse's coat.

Gymkhana – A mounted-games competition.

Hands high (hh) – The units used to measure the height of a horse or pony. One hand equals 4in (10cm).

Headcollar – A collar which buckles around the horse's head, so he can be led or tied up.

Hoof – A horse's foot.

Hoof pick – A hook used to clean mud and stones out of a horse's hooves.

Horse show – An event where horses and riders compete at showing, and sometimes jumping or mounted games.

Horses – This can be used generally, to mean both horses and ponies. Or it can be used more strictly, to mean only larger horses (higher than 14.2hh).

Jockey – Someone who rides racehorses.

Jodhpurs – Stretchy leggings made specially for riding.

Mane - The hair along the top of a horse's neck.

Mare - A female horse or pony.

Markings - White patches of hair on a horse's face or legs.

Mounting - Getting on a horse.

Mucking out - Cleaning the horse's stall or stable.

Neckstrap - A strap which buckles around a horse's neck, giving his rider something extra to hold onto.

Ponies - Small horses (14.2hh or under).

Reins - Part of the bridle. They are the long straps that you hold.

Riding school - A place where instructors teach people to ride.

School - An enclosed space used for riding lessons.

Seat - A rider's position in the saddle.

Showjumping - A sport where horses and riders jump a series of fences in an arena.

Showing - A sport where horses are judged on their appearance and manners, and the way they move.

Stallion - A male horse or pony, generally used for breeding.

Stirrups - The parts of a saddle which support a rider's feet.

Tack - Saddles and bridles.

Tacking up - Putting the saddle and bridle on a horse.

Three-day event - A competition which covers dressage, showjumping and cross country.

Untacking - Taking off the saddle and bridle.

Western riding - A style of riding using long stirrups, with the reins held in one hand.

Some of the myths and stories in this book contain tricky names. This is how to say them (the parts of the words in **bold** are stressed).

Bellerophon - Bell-**air**-oh-fon

Chimaera - Kim-**ear**-a

Helios - **Hee**-lee-oss

Odin - **Oh**-din

Phaeton - **Fay**-et-on

Philonoe - Fill-oh-**no**-eh

Rakush - **Rark-sh**

Rustam - Roos-**tom**

Sleipner - **Slape**-near

Zeus - **Z**-yuse

Acknowledgements

Edited by Lesley Sims. American editor: Carrie Armstrong.
Artwork for pages 58-61 by Katie Lovell. Digital manipulation by John Russell.
Managing designer: Mary Cartwright.

Every effort has been made to trace the copyright holders of the material in this book.
If any rights have been omitted, the publishers offer their sincere apologies and will rectify this in any
subsequent editions following notification. The publishers are grateful to the following organisations
and individuals for their contributions and permission to reproduce material:

Pages 2-3: Mare and foal © Mark J. Barrett/Alamy. **Pages 6-7:** Wild horses © Jeff Vanuga/CORBIS. **Pages 8-9:** Pony
© Kit Houghton; White horse © Horsepix; Horse family © John Conrad/CORBIS. **Pages 10-11:** Welsh pony © Horsepix;
Appaloosa © Bob Langrish; Arab © Bob Langrish; Thoroughbred © Horsepix; Andalucian © Bob Langrish; Shetland pony
© Renee Morris/Alamy; Shire horse © Bob Langrish. **Pages 12-13:** Two white horses © Manfred Grebler/Alamy;
Horse and girl © Royalty-Free/Corbis. **Pages 14-15:** Girl with pony © Jeff Greenberg/Alamy. **Pages 16-17:** Saddled pony
© Horsepix. **Pages 22-23:** Girl riding © Horsepix. **Pages 24-25:** Jumping over log © The Photolibrary Wales/Alamy.
Pages 28-29: Shetland ponies © Kevin Schafer/CORBIS. **Pages 30-31:** Girls at competition © Martin Rogers/Getty Images.
Pages 32-33: Mounted games © Trevor Meeks/Horse and Hound; Thanks to Ros Evans of the Pony Club (Eglinton Hunt
Branch) for reference pictures of the Prince Philip Cup. **Pages 34-35:** Show pony © Bob Langrish; Western show © Bob
Langrish. **Pages 36-37:** Show jumping © Mike Hewitt/Allsport/Getty Images; Milton © Kit Houghton/CORBIS; Puissance ©
Michael St. Maur Sheil/CORBIS. **Pages 38-39:** Extended trot © Bob Langrish; Spanish Riding School © kolvenbach/Alamy.
Pages 40-41: Jumping © Kit Houghton; Riding through water © Horsepix; Badminton Poster © Kit Houghton. **Pages 42-
43:** Racing at St. Moritz © Bob Langrish; *Eclipse* (1770) by George Stubbs © Private Collection/Bridgeman Art Library.
Pages 44-45: "Black Beauty" © Horsepix. **Pages 46-47:** Coins courtesy of maltergalleries.com; Bucephalus © Araldo de
Luca/CORBIS; Babieca © Shaun Cunningham/Alamy; Animals in War memorial © Collections Picture Library. **Pages 48-
49:** Circus painting (1891) by Seurat (detail) © Edimédia/CORBIS; Liberty horses from *Cavalia* © 2004 Getty Images;
Buffalo Bill poster © Private Collection/Barbara Singer/Bridgeman Art Library; *Carmen* © Rowena Chowdrey/ArenaPAL.
Pages 50-51: Horse-drawn bus © Mary Evans Picture Library; Troika
© Mikhail Kondrashov "fotomik"/Alamy; Pony Express poster © Bettmann/CORBIS; Mounties © Tim Thompson/CORBIS.
Pages 52-53: *National Velvet* © MGM/The KOBAL Collection; *Black Beauty* © Bureau L.A. Collection/CORBIS; Marguerite
Henry and Misty courtesy of The Misty of Chincoteague Foundation; Wild horses © Nancy Greifenhagen/Alamy.
Pages 54-55: *Neptune's Horses* by Walter Crane (1910 colour litho of 1892 painting) © Bibliotheque des Arts Decoratifs,
Paris, France/Archives Charmet/Bridgeman Art Library; Unicorn (1602) by Domenichino (detail) © Alinari Archives/
CORBIS; White Horse of Uffington © Skyscan/CORBIS. **Pages 56-57:** Flying horse © Robert Harding Picture Library Ltd./
Alamy; *Whistlejacket* (1762) by Stubbs (detail) © National Gallery Collection, by kind permission of the Trustees of the
National Gallery, London; Horse sketches by Theodore Gericault (detail) © Christie's Images/Bridgeman Art Library;
Thelwell cartoon reproduced with the permission of Punch, Ltd./www.punch.co.uk; *Little Blue Horse* (1912) by Franz Marc
© Saarland Museum, Saarbrucken, Germany/Bridgeman Art Library.

First published in 2006 by Usborne Publishing Ltd.,
Usborne House, 83-85 Saffron Hill, London ECIN 8RT, England.
www.usborne.com